PRAISE FOR ORLANDO FERRAND

"Orlando Ferrand sees beauty."

—Oriol Gutierrez, editor in chief of *POZ Magazine* and curator for Visual AIDS Gallery

"Very moving and a pleasure to read . . . Ferrand is clearly a poet unafraid to share with readers his journey around New York and toward himself, and the result is often beautiful."

—Bernadette Acocella, 5-star review for *Reader's Favorite*

"Ferrand explores the human condition with depth akin to Pablo Neruda and W.B. Yeats. His words are like the fragile layers of a pearl, which must have contact with the skin, or they die. His poems collectively are a trail of sand we keep kicking into, breadcrumbs left in the forest. Consuming each one, a word bit by bit until we find our home together."

—Dianne Bowen, 5-star review for *Reader's Favorite*

"Insightful and raw . . . [Ferrand's] recognition of his self-worth cannot be contained or distracted by the city and its denizens. What a wonderful read."

—D.L. Bodero, 5-star review for *Amazon*

"Inspired me to write poetry of my own!"

—Charlie Vazquez, author of *Contraband*, Rebel Satori Press

"An amazingly gifted poet/writer . . . [We] were all looking for something bigger than ourselves. A direction in life, love, a purpose that would reveal itself in a late night encounter with a beautiful stranger or a moment of clarity, alone under the stars, looking over the Hudson River. Pretty brilliant stuff. I am a fan!"

—Linda Nieves-Powell, author of *Free Style, Simon & Schuster*

"The key to attracting readers is to give it that touch, that dose of magic entangled with your very own reality as troubled, as sour as that might be, which is what Orlando has always done in everything he sets out to do whether it is poetry, or fiction, or his take on the visual arts. It grabs you . . . You are enthralled, captivated by this magician who writes with his guts."

—Manuel A. López, author of *El arte de perder. The Art of Losing*, Eriginal Books LLC

"Even after God departed, living in the secular world also suggests the possibility of a rebirth of consciousness and a renewal of wisdom. The glance of the poet adulterates and deconstructs deceiving appearances. Can we sort out loneliness? Can sanity be recovered? Where is home? Let's find out as we delve in this archipelago of memories and fractured tales leading into the heart of the poet."

—Mildred Nicotera, literary critique for *Linden Lane Magazine*

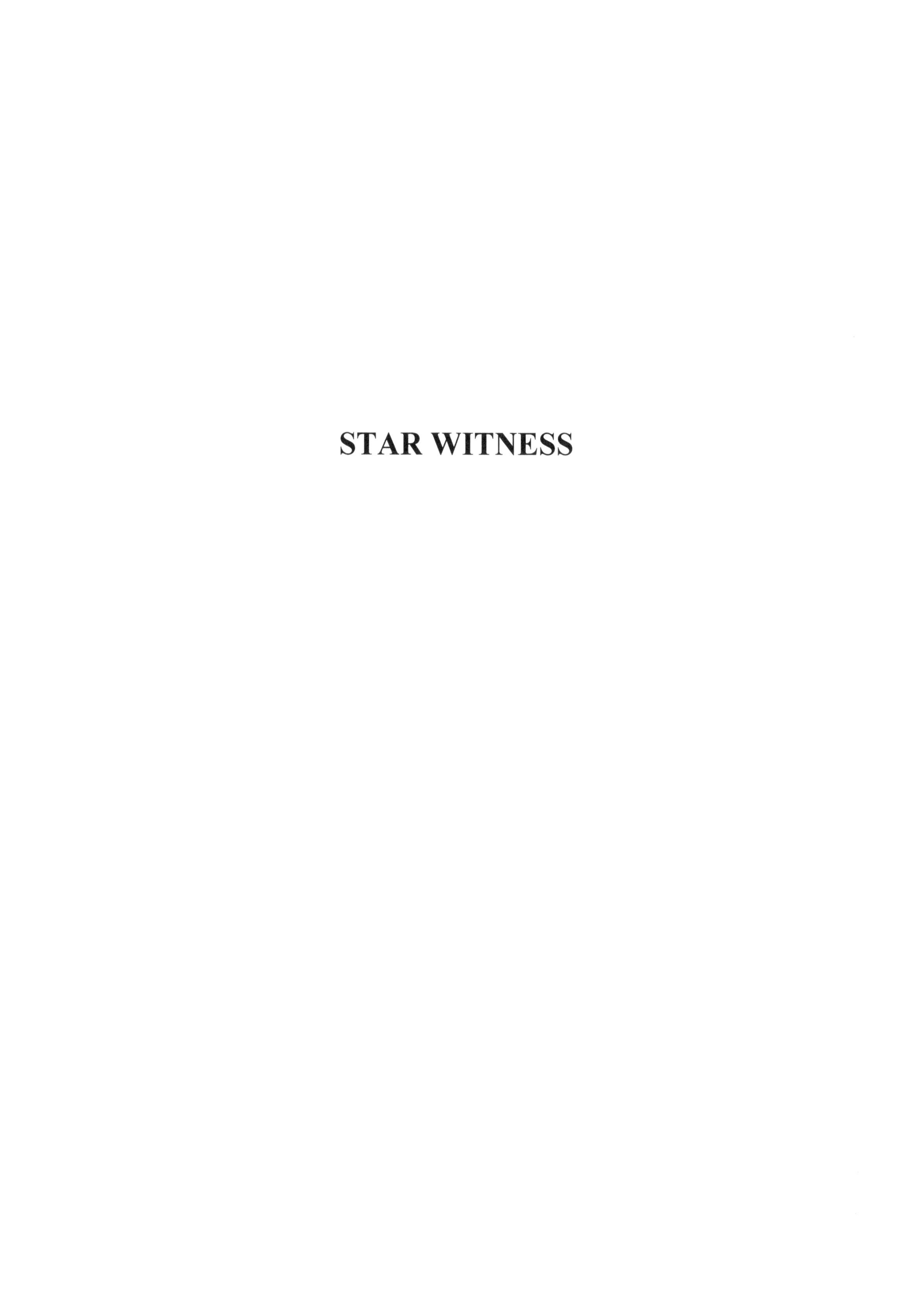

STAR WITNESS

Also by Orlando Ferrand in Print, for the Stage, and on the Web

POETRY

New Voices Anthology 2016 (edited by Raquel I. Penzo)
El péndulo
La otra Isla
The Best of PANIC! (Downtown New York/Latino Reading Series & Anthology curated and edited by Charlie Vazquez)
Citywalker

NONFICTION

Sookie in the Sky with Dreamers
Underneath the Accent of My Skin—TED Talk
Art AIDS America, Bronx Stories & Ofrenda/Offering: The Making of a Mass for Keith Haring & Angel
Sea, Ice-Cream, and Sex
Metaphors and Their Distemper Revisited: Meditation on My Reading at the Whitney Museum of American Art Presented by Visual AIDS
Home Beyond Vanishing Points
Apologia: Cuban Childhood in My Backpack

OPERA LIBRETTO

Still Life with Daniel, the Lonely Mutant

MASS

Ofrenda/Offering for Keith Haring & Angel

PLAYS

Requiem for Clay Gods
Ballad for Kangaroos
Narcissus
The Other Island

GRAPHIC MEMOIR

2000

BLOGS

Dancing with Muses (Blogger)
Pandora's Box is Open (Tumblr)

STAR WITNESS

Poetry

Orlando Ferrand

Preface by Robert F. Cohen, Ph.D.

CreateTank Press
New York

CreateTank
2420 Bronx Park East, Suite 6C
Bronx, NY 10467
CreateTank on Facebook
www.facebook.com/mycreatetank
Email: createtankmedia@gmail.com

2018 CreateTank First Edition
Star Witness

Book design: CreateTank
Cover design based on Orlando Ferrand's photograph of the Total Eclipse of the Sun observed from the rooftop of his residence in the Bronx, NY, on August 21, 2017.

To purchase a limited edition print of the Total Eclipse of the Sun, limited edition book cover design posters, limited edition artwork prints, and collectible-signed copies of *Star Witness* limited first edition hardcover, address orlandoferrand@orlandoferrand.net.

Author photograph: Jose Ramon Photography
www.gnoteentertainment.com

For information about exclusive discounts for bulk purchases, please email createtankmedia@gmail.com.

Orlando Ferrand is available for live events, recitals, lectures, and creative writing workshops. For more information or to book the artist and writer, please contact orlandoferrand@orlandoferrand.net.

Manufactured and printed in the United States of America

ISBN: 978-0-692-96390-6

ACKNOWLEDGMENTS

I am very grateful for the unwavering belief in my potential as a writer that my editor and mentor, Robert F. Cohen, Ph.D., has expressed on my behalf since the very first day we met when I was his student at Columbia University.

I am thankful to my poetry professor, Barbara Ungar, Ph.D., for sharing the poetic sensibility and wisdom that made me fall in love with poetry in her class at City College.

My most profound gratitude to the following publishers:

Belkis Cuza Malé, for publishing earlier versions of some of these poems in Linden Lane Magazine and *La otra isla*, Linden Lane Press, 2011.

Raquel Penzo (La Pluma y La Tinta), for publishing some of these poems in the *New Voices Anthology 2016* and for showcasing my work in her reading series and the 7th Annual New York Poetry Festival.

Charlie Vazquez, for publishing some of these poems in the anthology *The Best of Panic*, 2010 and for showcasing my work at the reading series, PANIC!

Carmen Karin Aldrey, for publishing an earlier version of "Pendulum" in *La Peregrina Magazine,* 2012.

I am eternally grateful to:

Joseph Carrión, Ph.D., for his editorial feedback on this manuscript in the making.

Edward Tatton, TEDx Organizer, for inviting me to present my TED Talk & Recital, *Underneath the Accent of My Skin*, in which several poems in this book were shared with an audience for the first time.

Esther McGowan, Alex Fialho, and Nelson Santos at Visual AIDS, for presenting my recital at The Whitney Museum of American Art and curating my series of landscape photography showcased during the performance.

TED Talks; The Whitney Museum of American Art; PEN America; Bronx Museum of the Arts; Rhina Valentin (Bronxnet); Lorraine Curreley (Poets Network & Exchange, Inc.); GNote Entertainment; Nita Noveno (Sunday Salon); Elyssa Goodman (The Miss Manhattan Non-Fiction Reading Series); Maria Meli; Chris Campanioni; Jessica Lanay Moore (Lost Lit & The Jasper Collective "Visitations" Reading); Karin Lundberg; Lucy Aponte (Poe Park Visitor Center); and Diamante Show (MNN) for hosting me.

New York State Council on the Arts (NYSCA); Lower Manhattan Cultural Council (LMCC); Creative Capital; Bronx Writers Center; Bronx Council on the Arts (BCA); Bronx Book Fair; Lehman Stages; and The Latina Book Club for their continued support.

For my mother Cary and my sisters Elizabeth and Marisol
(my three muses)

For Joseph
(when we shared the same colors of our dreams)

and in memory of

Sookie

Contents

Readers of *Star Witness* will think that they have entered a house of worship when they embark upon the reading of Orlando Ferrand's extraordinary book. I say house of worship because in such an environment, we all feel safe. Within the protective buffers provided by its walls, in this atmosphere of compassion and understanding, not only can we freely confess to our darkest and innermost secrets, but we can also liberate ourselves from the weight of problems that have tortured our soul. Because it is clear to us that we will not be judged, we can go public with our most private yearnings and, at the same time, rejoice in the sanctity of life.

It is precisely in his struggle to "reconcile the good and evil in [his very own] temple" ("Aurora") that Orlando Ferrand takes us, in *Star Witness*, on a moving personal journey. The book, orchestrated through the "crafting" of works resonating with "benedictions [and] maledictions," as forecast in "Nephila," the introductory poem, comes to life through the weaving of tales that show both the light and dark moments that contribute to the contours not only of his existence but ours as well. The poet's stark candor permits him to create an intimate bond with the reader. Whether he is writing about his own personal experiences or the experiences of others – actual friends and family members, famous artists, sculptors, and writers, unknown individuals to whom he gives a name, celebrated military leaders and legendary mythological and biblical figures embodying our historical and cultural past – the reader will identify well with these themes that give substance to his artistry.

Among the "benedictions" to which he alludes, Mr. Ferrand writes eloquently about the joy of being loved and of giving one's love, the comfort one feels in finding solace in the beauty of nature, and the ecstatic heights to which one ascends when blessed with true happiness in a world of kindness and generosity. As for the "maledictions" that he describes, Mr. Ferrand strives through his portrayals to eradicate the pain one feels when being molested and victimized by sexual or verbal abuse, when having to abort the life of a child conceived in rage, when being addicted to drugs, seen as a social outcast, and being subject to mere greed. One cannot help but become more hopeful and more socially conscious when imbibing the sweet splendors of the poet's "magical kingdom" ("Honey") and considering the bitterness of his biting social commentary. As the powerful thrust of these universal themes propels the poet forward in his journey, the reader becomes his loyal companion.

In this close-knit partnership, the reader also learns that a critical aspect of the poet's effort is reflected in the work he is doing on his own self-development. The more one reads *Star Witness*, the more one realizes how central to the poet's role as visionary, or "star witness," is his quest for self-knowledge. It is interesting to observe how this part of his journey is often most apparent when seen against the backdrop that the poet creates through his references to time and space. As the "star witness," and principal observer, his vision across time – past, present, and future – is all-pervasive. Yet, through his "prophetic eyes," time remains "old and eternal" ("Visitor") and, as an "abstract friend [r]efusing to be measured by the ticking of the clock" ("Exile"), sometimes even stops ticking as the divisions between the past, present, and future become blurred. Space, like time, is also an abstract phenomenon that is loosely determined in his universe. For while he travels through intergalactic spaces, shooting for different stars like a bird that "never leaves the air" ("Q & A With the Sphinx"), he does not seem to find a true home or "anchor" on Earth other than, perhaps, the "wisdom of life" ("Home Revisited"), which he hopefully discovers "in the man inside [himself]." As a result of his continual pursuit of knowledge by "look[ing] inward" ("Magnum Opus"), the poet seems to achieve a good sense of self in "Star Witness," the last poem of the volume, where he appears to be transformed and ready for the possibilities of a new life:

This morning
is an awakening.

Like a butterfly hovering under the first ray of sun
I embrace
my resurrected
heart.

Thus, as the book comes to a close, the poet no longer views himself as "[a] mirror [s]howing [him] the face [he] cannot see" ("Buddha Mio"). For both him and the reader, all the elements of optimism – a new day, a new soul, a new heart – are there for a new beginning, and this is a true "benediction."

Elements of Style: How the Content Translates into Form

To appreciate how Mr. Ferrand succeeds in telling us this story, it is important to explore what he does in order to sustain the reader's enthusiasm. First of all, each poem is an "organism" unto itself that takes on a life of its own and assumes a pattern that is particular to its very own needs. Because the formats change, the reader never gets bored and remains excited when going from work to work. This has been made possible, perhaps, because throughout the creative process the poet has liberated himself from the "required norms" of poetry writing by treating each topic as he sees fit.

There is even a whimsical quality to the attention the poet gives to this aspect of his presentation. For instance, the poem "Hanging from Your Thread" actually appears one word at a time, like a "thread" of words on several pages, and it is fun for the reader to read. When, in "Nephila," the spider "spins above the roses, the birds, and your own head," it is quite refreshing for the reader to see "spins above" written accordingly:

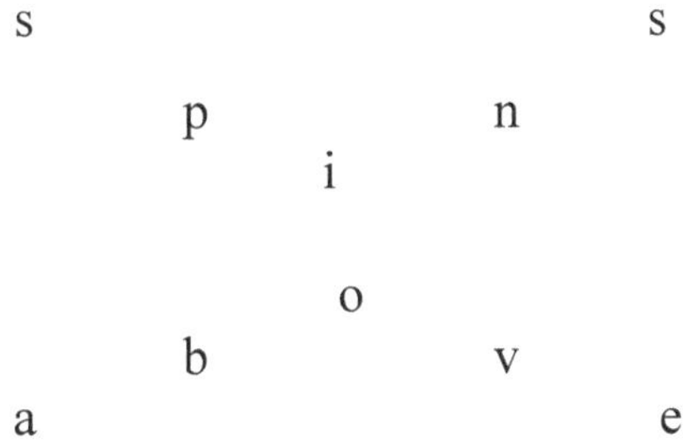

The poet implements the same kind of approach in different ways for words like "drop," "descends," and "falling" in the poem. His technique is effective because at each step the reader is able to visualize how springy the movements of the spider are. Indeed, in this regard it is difficult to overlook Mr. Ferrand's affinity with E.E. Cummings, who treated many of his poems as if they were visual objects on the page.

It is no coincidence that Mr. Ferrand has exploited the advantageous impact of these visuals. Although his creative genius belies definition, one might call him an expert in the "plastic arts" because his artistic aspirations have not been limited to poetry alone. He has also worked quite seriously as a painter, sculptor, graphic artist, photographer, and cinematographer throughout his career, and has borrowed from all these modes of expression in the creation of this book of poetry. Again, in "Nephila," when the words on the page take on a "rubber-band quality," it is almost as if the poet himself has explored the proper tension that needs to be applied so that each letter will land flat, right on the page. In the same poem, the work of the cinematographer also takes hold:

Panic
if her whole web
d
        e
                s
c
                e
        n
d
        s
landing on you
like a broken parachute

Imagine how successful the poet is here. His analogy – "like a broken parachute" – comes to life because the reader "sees" – as if in a moving picture – the spider web's unraveling occur during the spider's fall. Clear from the picture painted is how very much like the spider web's own dismantling is that of the parachute as the parachutist falls to the ground. Mr. Ferrand the cinematographer, with the support of the other inner resources contributing to his creativity, his other "eyes," the eyes of the painter, the graphic artist, and the photographer, makes this happen, and the image remains firmly fixed in the reader's mind way after he or she has focused on it.

That Orlando Ferrand is a scientist is therefore quite apparent. I say scientist because I believe all good poets are scientists. I use the word broadly because, based on its Latin root, a "scientist" is "someone who knows." To be a good poet, an individual must be able to write sound analogies and create metaphors, and unless he or she has investigated how things work, he cannot do so because he cannot compare things accurately and invoke these relationships through words. In this light, it should not be too much of a stretch for me to say that Mr. Ferrand is very much like a scientist in his approach to his writing. His personal affinity with sculpture as a medium, for instance, permits him to make appropriate references to clay and stone in such poems as "Camille Claudel: Interior Soliloquy Carved in Stone," "I Sing to Stone," and "Clay Whisper." In these "environments" he is not just a poet, but a poet "speaking" like a sculptor. In the same vein, it is because of his great knowledge of history, art, geography, archeology, literature, mythology, philosophy, religion, pop culture, and so forth that he is able to create poems that are not only rich in vocabulary and imagery but whose appeal always makes the issues discussed real and palpable for the reader even when the story being told is couched in an epoch far removed from the contemporary one.

The commitment he has made in order to achieve this result is therefore quite impressive because we cannot appreciate Mr. Ferrand's final product without imagining the homework that he must do at all times in order to be "someone who knows." For instance, for the poem "The Fool on Bronx Park East," he undoubtedly did quite a lot of research in order to master the vocabulary that describes all the parts of an umbrella. The twenty underlined words in the verse shown below, all parts of an umbrella, reveal how erudite and conscientious a writer he is:

And I am left alone
with <u>the nose-cap</u>, <u>the collar</u>, <u>the tip cup</u>
<u>the hand-spring</u>, <u>the tube</u>, <u>the runner</u>,
<u>the inside rosette</u>, <u>the stopper pin</u>, <u>the stretcher</u>,
<u>the tip</u>, <u>the rib</u>, <u>the tie</u>,
<u>the prevent</u>, <u>the inside cap</u>, <u>the notch</u>,
<u>the outside rosette</u>, <u>the open cap</u>
<u>the fit-up</u>, <u>the ferrule</u>, <u>the rosewood handle</u>
The Umbrella, parachute to help me land
has grown its skin again; it's not a fragile frame.

Through this dynamic litany of words, the poet has given to the umbrella, a simple object that we often take too much for granted, a new life and the dignity that it deserves.

Remarkably, in the penultimate line of the above verse, the image of the "parachute" reappears, and I must return to the poem "Nephila" one more time. When I first started reading *Star Witness*, I foolishly believed that Mr. Ferrand himself had invented the name "golden silk orb-weaver" for the purposes of his book. Soon after doing my editorial research, I found that "golden silk orb-weaver" is actually the English equivalent for the Latin term *nephila* spider. Pardon my naïveté! As a result of my discovery, I came to admire Mr. Ferrand all the more because what he does with "Nephila," the book's introduction, is to set the tone for the book's further unfolding by creating a double-entendre that takes us from the concrete to the abstract.

In concrete terms, the "golden silk orb-weaver" produces large orb webs with yellow spider silk; although it is not poisonous, it leaves a burning sting after biting a person. However, in abstract terms, one can readily think of these three narrative elements coalescing in Mr. Ferrand's work: the tales from all over the world ("orb") that the poet weaves in order to tell the world his story, the sting that he gives to the reader so that the reader will be alert enough to listen, and the bright golden sun that inaugurates an "awakening" at the end of the journey. With such a brilliant tapestry woven into the movement of *Star Witness*, it is difficult to imagine that Orlando Ferrand could have started his book in any other way.

On the Nature of this Collaboration

It is not every day that a teacher has the rare opportunity to write in depth about a former student years after they first met in the classroom. Surely one cannot hope to be accorded such an honor more than once in a lifetime. Orlando Ferrand was a student in an advanced writing class that I taught in the evening at Columbia University in July 1993. On the day after the first class, a day on which the class did not even meet, Orlando came to see me in quest of a more comprehensive reading list. While I was photocopying materials for another class I was scheduled to teach on that day, there he was at my side in full "military" gear, wearing a black beret and army fatigues, with big black boots trailing up his legs. I stood at attention.

Little did I know that that very event would mark the birth of a cherished friendship, blessed all the more by the fact that we have each assumed on one another's behalf at different times throughout the years the supportive roles of student, teacher, mentor, and editor. Since that auspicious moment, I have seen Orlando's "militancy" in action, a militancy that has provided him the will to break down whatever barriers have stood in his way in order to be able to realize his dream: to live his life as a creative artist. That he has met his goal is quite an achievement for any of us to fathom, and I could not be prouder of him.

I started working with Orlando on *Star Witness* in the fall of 2015. I had edited his prose writing before, most notably the work he did on *Apologia: Cuban Childhood in My Backpack*, his moving memoir, and when working on Orlando's prose, I had done my editing for the most part within my own "silent" domain. However, in my mind a different approach was warranted in the editing of his book of poetry. When embarking upon this project with Orlando, I suggested that the scope of our collaboration needed to reflect a combination of my own "silent reading" as the editor and his more "vocal" recitations as the poet. With his agreement to this recommendation, Orlando recited his poems out loud each time we met for a period of about eight months. The desired result was achieved: At the same time that I read his poems, I "heard his voice." Arduous as it was, this technique was very effective. As we listened to the phrasing and cadences of each poem, along with the internal rhythms and images that bring each one to life, we were able to make certain modifications to content and form that improved the manuscript considerably.

A teacher can have no greater joy than that of seeing a student prosper and thrive. In my case, this joy has extended far beyond what is normally expected because I continue to have the privilege of keeping in touch with Orlando Ferrand on so many different levels. In fact, as I have already suggested, for my own writing efforts we have also switched roles because he has served as my mentor and editor on many occasions. To be sure, the gift of such an exchange is priceless in value.

I am most grateful to Orlando for the opportunity he has given me to work on this project with him, and I am so pleased with the final product. Readers of *Star Witness* will hear Orlando Ferrand's voice come through loud and clear in each poem without requiring a recording from him. And among the many emotions that they will experience is one that I had when editing this book: While reading Orlando Ferrand's *Star Witness*, readers will be made to feel "whole again" ("Honey").

Robert F. Cohen

Star Witness

NEPHILA *1*

The spider
a golden silk orb-weaver
consecrates the steps of the wanderer

The spider
a golden spider
will disarm the hunter

The spider
a golden silk orb-weaver
s   s
          p   n
                    i

                    o
          b   v
a   e

the roses
the birds
and your own head

The gypsy's magic carpet
has been hewn
by the golden silk orb-weaver

And she returns the favor
by offering the spider
her treasured hidey-holes

Be not afraid
for she could

d
          r

          o

          p

in front of you

Like a thirsty mirror
tipping the scales against misfortune

The spider
a golden silk orb-weaver

Panic
if her whole web
d
e
s
c
e
n
d
s
landing on you
like a broken parachute

Your golden age is over

The spider
Nomad, Fairy and Witch
will always be alive

In our treasured timeworn legends
In the horror tormenting the child
locked in a dark room
In our precious handmade gardens
In the houses we dare not name
In the insanity hoarding the belongings
of our dear departed
In the relative estranged from all
In the courtesan and the hustler
too detached to love

Beware of the spider
when playing hide and seek

Beware of the spider
in rituals without faith

Beware of the spider
and the infinite web of greed

3

Beware of the venom
that sustains the spider
like ancient stardust words
feeding our cherished fairy tales

Beware of the spider

In the dreamer's dream

The spider
a golden silk orb-weaver
Crafting your benedictions or maledictions.

HOME REVISITED

When homing pigeons fly over my sky
and I don’t care,
a man can’t find his heart
in a broken city corner
a man is severed from his shadow

Pegasus
announces the season
when simple, minute gestures
become a necessity to sustain the soul
those simple, little things, my friend
again, the simple little things

I’m soaked in rain dancing with Eliot
in the cruelest of all months
Time is that man who every morning
tattoos a new heart on his chest
a man
who learns how to wait

And allows the water to shelter him
to carry him like one carries the wounded Christ
Let the bells dance to the breeze of life
Let the light shine
to scare sadness away from home
my friend
away from home

Let us take a seat at the table
we don’t have to wait for the messenger to arrive
Let us embrace the day when you will come closer to me
so we can tame the world
the day my door
the only door, will forever be open
the door to the man’s heart
the man himself, my friend
the man inside yourself

Let us embrace that day
when bridges
will be built across galaxies
and extinguished animals
will look at us
as if we had mastered the wisdom of life.

VISITOR

for Eliseo Diego

The voice of memory speaks falling from his white head
his mannerisms detach from that habitual closeness to familiar certainties
and the shadows remain hostages
of silent thieves trespassing his hideaway
a cave of bountiful deeds.

We violate the house of the most lucid host
and scare the spirits, his hidden visitors, away

We sneaked into his home
not knowing that its corridors
were routes of snow
guiding the eternal calmness of the children
born under the mighty touch of God.

He is here

Softly kissed by a legion of angels,
coming out of his top hat as if claimed by street magicians
without haste,
lingering
to let us in on the other side of life
since life has lost today its soothing outlines.

Whilst the ancient dust of wizards
disappears from his hands, painted by El Greco
ever straining forward to reach the light we cannot see
from this other side of life
and witness time grow old in his prophetic eyes
old and eternal
as only time can be.

TALE OF ORLANDO & VIRGINIA WOOLF

A phantom woman in slow motion waves at me
She is of the age in which stones crumble into dust
As frail as a naked angel disguised by Bosch
"Virginia" —introducing herself—
Walks right into my life

Deceiving the game of gender,
Orlando had to dress and undress eternally in front of the mirror
Seasons turned centuries have come and seasons gone
But never before the touch of a woman named Virginia
Had shaken identity and creed

Looking at the lighthouse with pebble-filled pockets
Shipwrecked by the burden of insanity and tedium
Shouting "I am your maker, Orlando!"
Virginia crosses to the other shore
Anointing the child with the wisdom only known to poets and suicides.

CAMILLE CLAUDEL: INTERIOR SOLILOQUY CARVED IN STONE

I'm carrying the weight of
Loneliness
As I once carried suitcases filled with the bone and blood of
My statues.
I lost my stiletto shoes twirling on the streets like an intoxicated Cinderella,
I ran though the metro in Paris, cursing at you, all of you,
Impostors,
Masters of mediocrity.
My slithering tongue will be a constant reminder of
All the reasons why
You won't be remembered,
At least not as much as I.

Do not pretend to worry about my disappearances.
Those times when I vanish
I'm just a little girl sculpting a doll out of clay
In a dark room.

I'm looking at you from that timeless space
Which defines the
Absolute.
You see?
You were all jealous of a benevolent God
I didn't even believe in.
He gave me
What you couldn't fathom
In your hubris.
You kneeled down in front of masterpieces
Named after virgins and
Saints.
In reality,
They were echoes of beauty and lust
Trapped
Inside
And then,
Unleashed
From my body
By the simple touch of
Clever
Eyes.

Oh mother, mother,
You are nothing
But a sack of rotten potatoes.
You look your best right there
In the portrait
With veins of oil,
As your eyes roll up
Always hating.

Dust has accumulated on the windowsills with fury
And for the first time in Eternity I feel sorry for you,
Woman,
Living off royal delusions
That made a phantom of
You
Mother,
You confined me to your putrid uterus
So I could never see the light of
My spirit
Dancing
With all I ever had
My hands,
Bearing the secret of all stones
My
Hands.

I don't blame you. You envied my womanhood.
You didn't have the talent to fulfill
The only duties expected from you.
Motherless bitch. Frigid wife.
I absolve you.

Is that you?
Funny that they only remember you as my brother
And not as a writer
Or a great man,
Paul.
You could have saved me,
You could have loved me just a little
To open back the door to the world
You could have loved me just enough
To rescue me from the *Asile de Montdevergues*;
That was not meant to be my permanent home,
But your own fear kept me there.

You will never know love

Neither you, nor my decrepit lover
Rodin
Who made me a concubine at seventeen;
My petrified obsession,
The old man I carved in stone
And gave him the eternal splendor he never had

I tried to chisel you out of my heart
Like the tumor you know will kill you
But you are too afraid to surrender to the scalpel
I can't forgive myself
I am falling for a thief

Auguste,
I am your kidnapped muse
You murdered my life source
In the frenzy of every orgasm
Rodin,
The man who couldn't choose me over the other gals
Auguste Rodin,
Who tried to keep me frozen in marble veins.

In the moonlight, I run under the spell of Eric Alfred Leslie Satie

Paul,
Mom,
Sis,
Of the broken beyond repair
Camille Claudel,
You waited for father to die
To unleash the perpetual punishment
Crafted in the web of odium, disgust and aversion
Of your crippled god;
Inept at taming the temper of Camille
He sequestered me
Like a stolen relic
In the eternal looting
Of your own Catholic curse.

My house is flooded. Running for their lives,
My cats are climbing the poles
Still holding the ceiling like a wrecked sky.

The neighbors called me names,
They complained that I made too much noise,
That my home

Had slowly become a north-less ship in the Siena,
And they gathered around with torches
As if I were the bride of Frankenstein
Who'd just killed her child;

Indeed,
I did it before it had a chance to be born
It was like taking a crap
Push, push, and push.
I am laughing at all of you
Seduced by cheap bottles of Cognac,
My loyal lover,
A thin thread of unwoven blood
Squirts from
Underneath
My adolescent legs.
I am a crumbling Madonna like Mom
I expel the fetus out of my womb
Like a venereal disease
Before it kills me or makes me mad.

So burn me down, villagers!

They said I was a hoarder
One day I looked around and saw them,
My marble companions and their clay shadows
Ninety was too many of us
For that small house,
And I killed them too
I brought upon them my cataclysmic rage
Until
I turned them back
To dust

Time is leaving me now

There will be no tombstone
No resting place
Debussy will accompany my journey
As we walk into the fire

Silence, please!

Let me hear the lullaby
Mother earth will whisper in my ear
Claiming my bones until we fuse to the ground
And I become
Again
The finest of all clay.

ANGEL AND FARMER: QUEER REWRITING OF JACOB'S ENCOUNTER WITH THE ANGEL

A primeval smell of mahogany and peppermint
Solitude and idleness
Marriage equality and bliss
Trigger the capricious storyteller's mind
The stranger has arrived
And in his hands
The lime residue of Venetian walls

Behind the window, the stranger looks at the eternity of dreams
The dreamer dreams the dream of olden dreamers
His eyes are sieged by shadows in the night
The dreamer feels he's being watched

The beginning of the watches
The middle watch
The cock-crowing
The dawning

Until the night is lifted
And green-yellow fields of rice
Caressed from the Nile to the Euphrates
Gently touch the Angel's rosy skin

The flute's melody lures the young men
To glean the seeds of rice
The elderly sleep the siesta standing on their porches
Waiting on death as one waits on the departed lover
Dense is the light and dense the perfume
The Angel's scent
On the Farmer's hairy chest

The Angel's and the Farmer's lips
Will quench one another's thirst
The Promised Land will blossom
Rivers will bring the bounty to their hands
And in the dream of dreamers
The friendly wrestlers
Will wear the bronze-colored skin
Of Desert Wanderers

Angel and Farmer
Are under the spell of a forbidden fruit
Until the storyteller tastes on his lips
The concealed fable of Jacob's encounter with his Angel.

Q1: Where to anchor my eyes?
A1: Build no nest
Q2: How to appease the water that sheathes my forbidden island?
A2: Stretch your safety net
Q3: What borders will halt the fury of the wind?
A3: Become the bird that never leaves the air.

And the East and the West will christen
The city with a heavenly newborn
And the newborn will forever remain a child
And the newborn will allow all creatures in his kingdom
To satiate their thirst
by drinking water from his own cupped hands
And the newborn will heal all infirmities
He will rub the feet of vagabonds
Where the Aquehung or River of High Bluffs
meets the sea of Paumanok
And loneliness will be disremembered
The locks on front doors
Will be filled with blood as a reminder
Of the danger of voids
And the inhabitants will dwell in communion
Without fear of aliens
And bread will be placed again
In the center of the table
And the child will lead them
And they will immerse their uncovered bodies
in The Fountain of Youth
And man will be again
His brother's keeper
And he will be born form all unions of love
And he will look
Inward
And he will know.

PENELOPE WITHOUT HIM

"Since the left shoulder weighs more,
he is there, entangled in the prison of his feet,
the idiot."
Jose Lezama Lima

Penelope stitches up her feeble wound,
the butterfly's mortality unravels the balance of her wings.
She's thoughtless about her fiction man,
her pain-man
her too-long-gone hero.
She weaves the astonishment
of the seducers before the glass doors
are shattered by the wind
whilst Summer ripens
the sweet grapes into wine.
Penelope, the clock's concubine
outlining her panties
does not deny her loss.
Like a child, perpetually crafting the ritual of her instincts,
she reckons the timeless freedom enslaved to this old tale
and commands the shadows to undress on the way home.
She draws her deck of cards
waiting for nothing, for no one, recalling a name
who's turned into The Fool Tarot card.
Vague and upside down
the idiot wants to push her world out of sight.
But Penelope winds up her patient, loyal clock
and weaves, and weaves again
the smell of galloping horse riders to her flesh.
She nourishes the wounded passerby
and weaves, forever more
a butterfly of love into an undying heart.

I'm dragging the familiarity of sorting out the world
Like a contended God
I envy the children in front of their first Christmas tree
Urgently breathing in only the magic
That descends upon the ginger houses like a parachute of whishing stars

The flesh is gone
I've been nailed to the air as scarecrows in summertime
I push the waters and dance with the branches of longstanding trees
I am able to look at mankind
Without fear of catastrophes

But I miss you
I'm watching over you now
I am the one that soothes you in the form of pleasant dreams
I am the one that accidentally makes you spill
Sleeping pills and painkillers in the toilet

I am the one that took your heart in my hand
And massaged it until you saw me in the white emptiness called death
No, you are not dreaming the toll of distant bells
I commanded you to go back and whispered in your ear
A new manual of instructions on how to live without me

Be gentle
Do not crave the company of others only in accordance to your own needs
Flow like waters without ceasing
Empty your thoughts
And grow old without greed

Let there be light
Look up and bask in this miracle called life
Let there be light
The sky has grown
Another dying star.

EXILE

Time is my tasteless abstract friend
Refusing to be measured by the ticking of the clock
Time is all I have
When I shut down my windows to the world

I am absent from familiar voices
My body will return someday to interstellar dust
Transient and secular
I will carry the seed of a new life into Heaven

Oh, my lighthouse
Precision envelops my crystal sword again
The prophets' mystery finally revealed
A man is also a cave made out of shadows and winged castaways.

for the N.Y.U suicides

Where is the diver's valor?
Which water pocket conceals his burden?
I left behind the Ivory Tower in every jump off the cantilever
Breaking diving records—my passport to college
Until New York
That rapist insomniac
Snatched me from self
They insistently rung my doorbell in the dorm on 9th and 3rd
On that morning
They had looked at me looking at them
All ears to the homeless' revelations in Washington Square Park
While running from the ghosts of my classmates' bodies
Cracked and smashed like watermelons
Sequestering the asphalt
Still lingering
Refusing
To
Depart.

They said
Suicide is contagious
I am a prime suspect
They asked me why I didn't jump like the others
Yet
If I was thinking about it
Yet
Voices?
Your voices
Piercing my dick like a Prince Albert jammed in a crowded mouth
And I tell them,
I will slaughter—no regrets
The pack of wild dogs dressed in blue like you
That dares to bark at my steps into the unknown
Disturbing my communion with the phantom of Bobst Library
Do you feel the draft? Can't you see this place is haunted?

PTSD diagnosis and I'm good to go on another mission
I collected signs of the Missing
In hopes that I would find them in my dreams
I followed the weathercocks

Facing the ever changing anatomy of Manhattan
Got stranded over and over again
I brought 'em back to life from their escapades
To unmapped expanses
"We are waiting for you"
And I keep holding my legs tight to the ground to no avail
Begging other apparitions to share my loaf of bread in their presence
Why is my mother tossing her Bible into the fireplace?
Why is her Christ bleeding from the cross in her fresh linen?
Why is her lunatic God flooding her house with myrrh and thorns?

I'm diving
Into the region where sailboats will never find me
I'm diving
My other island will finally emerge.

SKATERS IN THE NIGHT

Once again the skaters drain the breadth of time
I meander
Cosmic puzzle raising the sails on the boat
Like a mirror held up to reality when I can't shut eye.

Skaters,
This is the way of the time traveller
Remote creature
Fabricating his mystic tinsel.

Earlier
The dweller was thinking about nesting
In the space of solitude
Naked as an uttered word against the swiveling wind.

I balance my weight in vertical crossovers
I slide
World-on-wheels
Under my cobblestone-hunting feet.

Everywhere
Intergalactic glockenspiels are going to sound my name
And the Equinox will burst into
My age of precarious equilibrium.

Skaters,
I avert you in the nights
When the knifc-sharpened edge of my wheels
Unveils the footprints left by ancient rocketeers.

IN THE FUR OF THE WOLVES

They are pitfalls
Carpenter,
From this point on
The signs do not have any meaning
For you, that is

Eluding all warnings
You have become invisible to Daddy God
Forever mortal
The Son,
Undressed among the wolves

There is no going back
There is no possibility
Of biblical parole
The cross is in the making
Thy signs are being coined.

HELIOPOLIS

There was once such a place
Where the sun was worshipped
As any god
Before there was a god
Before God
Acquired so many faces
Languages
And was kidnapped
By religion and prophets
Crafting political upheavals
Out of avarice and sanctimoniousness
Yes, there was a place
Before God's words were meticulously carved
In stone
And thousands,
Perhaps millions of mortals
Were sold, enslaved, raped, stoned
To death
In the name of bloodthirsty laws
Protecting, as usual,
The rich from the destitute
There was once such a place
Where the sun was worshipped
City of On
In the cataclysmic biblical testaments
Beth Shemesh
As witnessed by Isaiah, Ezekiel, Jeremiah
The town where Moses learned all his wisdom
From the Egyptians
And Joseph became an architect of dreams
In Pharaoh's darling chambers
On the north-east bank of the Nile
Near Memphis and Cairo
There was once such a placc
Where Cleopatra's needles
Were erected into the sky
To poke the skin of the sun
God Atum-Re
With unfulfilled dreams, wonder
And questions full of fear
About the meaning of life
Before the prophecy
Announced an indefinite total eclipse of the sun

For the imminent future of mankind
There was a place named
Beth Aven
Where lordship and bondage were born
Yes, there is still such a place
Our city
Sustained
By the love of money, lust and the blood of slaves
The same city of cyclical returns
Safeguarded by the unchanged fallen angel at its feet.

And cities were conquered
That means
Women and kids raped
Monarchs beheaded
Husbands, uncles, brothers, and parents
Slaughtered

A bloody sea retreated and trapped the sky
Leaving us with that almost invisible
Vanishing hairline-word Horizon
It keeps giving us hope,
And the certainty
That we could sail away
If we don't like it here in the mean streets
On the island, in the desert, in the mountains
Or the ruins of our ransacked
Conurbation

The Magi unweave the threads
Into free prophetic whispers
A cosmic messenger
For the awaited child is on the way
Descending from the heavenly ladder
Directly connected to Mary's womb
Like an intergalactic aquarium
And he's swallowed by her black hole
As he obeys the direct command
Of the Master,

"I am impotent;
plant my seed in the girl—she is ovulating.
Using the method I showed you,
I will grow my begotten.
Make sure you take my sperm
directly into her cervix, the fallopian tubes,
or her uterus.
It makes the trip shorter for the sperm,
Are you listening, Apollyon?"
"Yes, Sir!"
"It will bypass any possible
obstructions. They've gotten out of hand.
We need to regain control
of the experiment.

Do as I say,
and I might let you back
In Heaven's think-tank."

The child will also be programmed to become a rebel
That means
He will fight his own kind first
Play with friends in the woods
And love them all:
The whore, the thief, the sex offender, the madman,
The terrorist, the fascist and the communist
He will love them all
And lay his life for
All

The blind can only see the light of his own steps

The rebel
surrounded
by angels
bearing golden
spurs was nailed
to the cross before time became an abstraction
for romantics, a temporary space without windows
to escape from, Time, the seed of life itself, here, as it is
everywhere
the wind
blows
over
magical
feasts
while we are
still waiting for that
promise
of
return.

THE WARRIOR

I claim ascension for the bird and for the man
When madness rings my doorbell
I won't answer. I am not here.
I ran away with the Samurai

At six, and for a very long time
The Japanese were my favorite action flicks
I loved to watch the black and white
Wind
Splashed
With blood,
Heads bouncing off
Bamboo trees,
The blade
Making with finesse
A vertical trajectory
From head to toe
In my enemy's
Body

Kidnapped
Japanese princesses
On the back of white horses
By those men who spoke fast and hard
And you couldn't really tell if they were
Loving or hating,
Just like Dad

I loved the sound effects
Cascading in infinite waves
Of ocean breeze,
And the smell of Sushi
In his breath,
My childhood friend,
The Samurai

Akira taught me
How to make
The sword dance in
My hands

He also showed me how
Warriors could turn into lovers
At the onset of light

He covered the mirrors at nightfall
To protect me against the phantom lady
From another world
Who waited patiently
Until I fell asleep
To take me away
And suck me dry
Like a ripened mango

We flew on the back of dragons
On those days when the house of my ancestors
Was plundered by Cuban monarchs
In uniform,
Screaming and holding
The Russian flag,
Spitting out centuries of unsustainable
Hunger and bloodbath

When Dad's Communist Party boss
Held my head against his chest
And gently forced me
Down on my knees,
"I'm gonna make a man out of you, boy.
Take it all the way
To the back of your throat
And swallow."
He said asking me to kiss it first
On Friday nights

Or when Diazepam
Rendered my mother
Into a rubber doll
Motionless cocooned in the wings
Of yellow butterflies
Crashing on the kitchen's granite floor
Enchanted, a lotus princess drowning
In white thick viscous silky vomit pond

When, accidentally, she set the house on fire
From mattress to backyard
By the slip of a burning cigarette hanging loose
From her mouth, she, too, was accustomed to swallowing

The Communist's gentle pushdown
Head to knees

Akira left when rainy seasons
Accompanied by starless nights
Were woven into the iron bars
The world had placed around me
To protect its ruthless inhabitants
From the fury and vengeance of
My sword

He said he would come back for me
After I had conquered the only thing
Worth living for, since hara-kiri was not an option,
The only thing left for Samurai to do
After all Japanese action flicks
Ended in mayhem and I had just turned
Thirteen

My spirit.
True to his promise
He came back for me
Transfigured into the wisdom
And good fortune dragon
Melting the iron bars
With tongues of fire

Fuku Riu touched me
With his three claws
And held me against
His slender serpent-like
Winged colorful body

And we became one
Wrapped in golden
Green and blue
Red and yellow skins
Ascending in the skies

We left behind
Treasure troves
The sword,
And our legend
Forever to be told.

ALEXANDER THE GREAT SPEAKS WITH THE SHADOW OF HIS DEAD LOVER HEPHAESTION

I do not want the throne, younger men, exotic women, or the riches
That every conquest will assure
My sword is now a gentle sight in the eyes of the enemy
You will return to my door and open your heart again
Silenced by disconcertment
Unease
You will find the exact gesture to console me
From the anxiety of those who have departed
And don't know it yet
You will find an angel carved in stone
With my bare hands
And you will come back every night
As usual
When our wives and guards are trapped in dreams of golden glory

A weeping willow grows inside my ribcage
The river shelters the solitary swan of Van Cortlandt Park

And your eyes will find me
And your voice will rapture in the wind
So I could hear you in the cardinal points missed by the compass

You will return to the Hanging Gardens of my Babylon
To our library in Alexandria where I still treasure the ceaseless poems
You wrote me defeating the legendary fires
You see
The flames of memories can shield against physical catastrophes

You will become that child again running wild with *cocuyos* in his hair
And you will love me

I will be waiting for you
Under the brutal snowstorm this time of year
And we will journey together to the most beautiful land
Ever seen by human eyes
And we will be enticed by the aroma of Jasmine
Impregnating the tropical evenings
Surrounded by the mountain range
Where Pines grow along the heat of Palm trees

You will come back to me
And witness
A man on his knees
Sowing seeds of wheat
While awaiting your return.

I SING TO THE STONE

On stone they have written
Legends
The commands of remote gods
The ambiguity of love
That cannot describe the feeling
of being at a loss
For words
They've killed
With a stone
And eternalized life
On stone
Sisyphus Stone
Falling
Down
In frothy innuendos
River stone
To appease the heat that sets me on fire
In those nights
Where the beautiful complexity of the moon
Crumbles in my traveler's hands
That touch
The stone
To give back
Its heart.

I was promised riches only matching Solomon's
And tropical pathways leading to eternal beauty and youth
They had promised me mirages never seen before

Treasures, which never hugged my hands
Until you arrived

Baptized in the river by John
With your blue smile
And your eyes of pure honey
Navigating my entrails

I want to be his sea
And his horizon
The rope that rescues his shipwreck

And the word Love
Shattering my veins

I want to be his friend
Sowing sunflowers
Adorning all the corners

When you return
To my hunter's arms
To my feet
Skilled in the art of mapping uncertain territories

Let's take a walk
When the evenings
Light the sky with rosy-orange-purple swirls

Listen to my voice
When I whisper magic words
Enticing the charm of life

Come
Let's dive now into the mystery

When the sea sustains us
Like gods fallen asleep
Soon awakening and recovering their memory.

CLAY WHISPER

He kneads me into an oval first
banged against walls and floors
until the wooden table collapses
under my solid mass of life
like your mother who never recovered
from the beatings I am
stretched beyond immeasurable distances
impossible things to be all the dragons
and witches and ogres and bad uncles
transient super heroes
while listening to the instructions
of the hysterical school teacher
touched by no one for more than 20 years
she hated toddlers and varicose veins
and the warm belly of your pregnant sisters
pastry moist with your sweat
sweet like Grandma's brown sugar cane lollypops
and ices sprinkled with Benadryl
just for color
in the absence of cherry extract
you are dozing over me
you are turning me into a womb
inside out hiding fragments of the pain
nobody sees but me no you are not
an ugly child troll your father got the gene
and will eventually die
of alcoholism don't worry keep making
more little everything out of me
stars and moons entire galaxies if you wish
to escape I don't like my off-white
color me wild like the nights you steal
from the trannies that give you more love
than anybody in this world your eyes travel
faster than the wind over the smooth texture
of this wholeness that I am
resuscitating again in the fire
galloping beneath your fingers
your smile finds my beaches of wild reefs

I'm stalking you   daydreamer *35*
illuminated on this lazy Susan
spinning at will
stretched into infinite perfection
giving birth to the sum of all things tangible
and impalpable
under your tears and occasional smiles
at last cocooned in your sculptor's hands.

SONNET FOR MARISOL

for my baby sister, whom I named

I will not run away from you ever
Again I come to you as I promised
Princess Marisol your heart is clever
My curse was sharp like glass against my chest
Stop Azrael from entering our home!
You brought the faith, the hope I had long lost
In geographies that made me waste my love
Thunder and fear trapped me in the frost
But now I learn how to draw the landscapes
To awaken your memories of me
And these holes on the earth's globe are my eyes
They look at everything anew, and see
My sun, my song, my life, my sea, my soul
My precious little gems, my Marisol.

MOMMA'S NEEDLE

The smell of saltpeter
And two hands kneading the bread
And my mother's voice
Weaving the wicker on my back
Out of my memories

With needles of the sky
Needles
That love and protect
Against the villains
In my tales

Needles
To crucify fear

Needles that safeguard
My descent to earth

Needles
To calm the madman
I have become

An exile inhabiting the coral reefs
Learning the language of the sea
So that the deep could venture
Into my home.

SEBASTIAN'S LAST ARROW

•

In this house
Mirrors are shattered
They fly
Blinded, smashed, the glass pieces
Opening my veins

And I escape
And ascend into Space
With the exact, extreme precision
Of the astronaut

I don't want to feel how fragile
My nights are

Picasso has the perfect colors

For my gestures
Broken

For my kisses
Scattered

In the wind

For my voice
Lifted

Beyond the weight of human gravity

For my hands
Seized by the brushes

Trying to retouch
One more time
My life
Before it haunts me.

BUDDHA MIO

I am the clown
Laughing
Crying under the nocturnal drizzle
Who will caress you with fury
Like a miscarried hurricane

I am the man who seeks love
The man who embraces
The ambivalence of friendship
A mirror
Showing me the face I cannot see

I am the little boy who hides
In the bushes of childhood
The traveler who will not spend another penny in transient love
I am the stone where the ego crashes
In the corners of New York

Oh, I am like Buddha
Far but not distant
Present but not omniscient
Fragile as Man
Eternal as God.

HONEY

Honey for the troubled. Give that kid some honey
Let him eat some honey and bathe in honey
Make him sweet with honey
Only honey can make him whole again.

Embrace him as if he were the sum of all goodness
you will ever have
Protect him from the very ones who gave him life
Honey, honey for the troubled.

Take a long train ride together
and allow him to scream for no apparent reason
in those places where nobody feels comfortable
and everybody senses the heavy weight of loneliness
because they have been deprived of the silliness
wrapped around the backpack of teenagers,
and the innocence of those who still believe
in the magical kingdom.

Fairies, Gnomes, Dwarfs,
Ghosts, Trolls, Dragons, Aliens,
Giants, Hare of Jade, Angels, Cyclops,
Demons, Evil Eye, Fauns, Genie,
Hombre del Saco,
Hydra, Leviathan, Medusa,
Hyperboreans, Ghouls, Mermaids, Nibelungs,
Golems, Nymphs, Oberon, Gorgons, Ogres,
Goblins, Orcs, Polyphemus, Remora, Ouroboros,
Salamanders, Scorpion Man, Sea Lions, Sphinx,
Unicorns, Elves, Leprechauns,
Spirits of all sorts,
Valkyries, Werewolves, Sylphs, Yeti, Sirens,
Vampires and Zombies.

Honey for the boy. Wet his handkerchief with honey
and accompany him in his travels
ending in sudden last stops,
in the back of train stations, red-eye flights.

Let him talk to himself,
play musical instruments with squatters,
walk through subway train cars preaching his own Gospel.

Honey for the madman. Let him claim his need for silence
against the metal buzz of derailed high-speed trains
and lost planes nose-diving in the ocean.

Honey, honey for the healing. Uncoil his rope from the ceiling
and help him turn it into an umbilical cord
Honey, honey for the healing. Don't let him leave again
and fight another war.

Honey for the troubled. Give that kid some honey
Let him eat some honey and bathe in honey
Make him sweet with honey
Only honey can make him whole again.

UNBOUND

You are nothing but the footprints of noise to my ears
I am that night when the ships in the Hudson
Will resist sailing for lost tourists
Where an imminent blackout will shut the city down
And planes will flutter in the air like acrobats suddenly realizing
There are no safety nets

No, I can't make up your words
Crackling
Our story was hijacked the moment you were
Seduced by your ghost companion in sickness and in health
Disguised as Crack, Meth, Angel Dust, Pot, Booze—garbage head
Your newly found pain on sale
And I ran for my life and made space for another me in the world

I'm still running
Running as this river where I almost drowned
Chasing mermaids back into their underwater gardens
So I could get away from you and me
Possessed by madness and suspense
Like characters in an Edgar Allan Poe story

I don't miss the after hours tipsy stroll down Christopher Street,
The public sex at the Piers, the circumnavigation of 8th Avenue,
The callback number on the beeper, my teenager whoever you are,
With my Blanche DuBois type of disposition
I have always depended upon the kindness of strangers

Nor do I miss that urge curiously linked to the obscenity of mortality:
The passing of close friends, our aging parents,
The agony of having to put to sleep the dying pets we love the most
Or the assumption that we were going to die young
Regurgitating in misery
With the loss of God

I don't miss your sudden bouts of lucidity
Climbing onto untimely moments in the night
That eventually would turn into another Dawn
Loaded with all those words I dare not say
And hugs lost like Diamond kites inside Cumulonimbus clouds

I have flashbacks and goose bumps
Witnessing derailed commuters during holiday seasons
When your phantom clings onto the surface of my mind
On Halloween
Inhabiting the adolescent vagabond
Blindly picking up cigarette butts from the asphalt
Assaulted by surprise in his helpless descent
On the solitary confinement of dead end streets
Under promised starry nights

Life has been gentle with me after all
All I had to do was bury you.

And
the
bells
will
toll
again
in
the
town
where
we
learned
how
to
kiss
for
the
first
time

I
will
be
here
absentminded
entangled
in
the
melody
of
those
sepia
toned
streets
where
elderly
ladies
in
their
youth
hypnotized
us
in

the
slipstream
of
their
perfume

They
are
still
knitting
into
their
wedding
dresses
the
habitual
gossip
the
secret
lives
of
married
men
mending
hope
and
resignation
with
every
stitch
of
their
grandchildren's
virginity

Ah!
those
streets
where
mothers
wished
their
sons
would
never
leave

home
aging
by
their
side
like
dried
prunes

But
I
left
town
and
quickly
learned
how
to
be
reborn
brutally
every
day
in
this
city
in
spite
of
my
insomnia
in
spite
of
escapades
in
NYC
parks
at
dusk
bath
houses
after
hours
spots
peepshows

and
sex
shop
back
rooms
in
spite
of
bewildering
holidays
where
the
Ace
of
Hearts
is
always
waiting
around
the
corner
tearing
apart
bonds
of
intimacy
like
a
common
thief

You,
Prince
Charming
of
my
delusional
loneliness
sheltered
under
the
flowers
offered
to
the
saints

for
answering
our
prayers

You
are
the
godforsaken
child
who
will
grow
up
fast
to
become
his
own
ruthless
tormentor

I
am
here
next
to
you
as
if
in
a
soap
opera
where
the
hero
and
the
villain
will
love
each
other
“till
death

do
them
part”

I’m
here
trying
to
complete
this
puzzle
under
the
giant
loony
orange
moon
fortune
cookie
unveiling
the
sea
the
horizon
and
the
distant
mountain
range
in
the
arras
of
the
sky

I
want
to
be
with
you
in
spite
of
the

danger
of
loving
others
more
than
we
appreciate
the
sanctity
of
life

Sickening
love
worse
than
heroin
withdrawal
for
the
addict

Today
when
the
Chinese
horoscope
predicts
my
shipwreck
and
the
word
love
drifts
through
my
fingers

I
am
here
and
the

fact
is
that
next
to
you
my
nights
and
days
light
and
shadow
the
emerging
regrets
for
those
and
everything
I
left
behind

My
mother
and
father
my
deceived
wife
and
children
the
kid
I
once
was
afraid
of
clowns
a
refugee
from
the
pain

and
agony
of
hopelessness
the
raptured
home
how
quickly
it
all
goes
away
if
I
am
next
to
you.

I have often wondered
Whatever happened to the stuff that escapes
My computer's memory
Like the only picture I had of my best friend
Taken just before he went to Iraq

You won't evaporate into Eternity
While I try restoring your image
In my scattered brain
Simulating the precision of a sniper

Nobody will ever know
That we wrestled on the sand
Of wild beaches
Visited by no one
That we read poetry to one another
Moonlit every weekend for years on end

Nobody will ever know
The taste of berries on your lips
That your eyes were fixed beyond the ocean
On those summer nights we spent on City Island

Nobody will ever know
How you really mastered
Your protuberant weapon in High School
Conquering the highest GPA

And you still left no trace behind
No family, no girl awaiting your return
No picture

However, beloved Xavier,
I have the certainty that you are now a cyber Argonaut

You exist in the non-time
Invisible matter to the human eye
Forever present
Secret.

SLEEPWALKER

If it were only always that easy
to embrace my circadian enemy
the one who broke my heart
after I brought him back to life
victim of his own self-inflicted violence

If only I could look at him in the eyes
He who knows my secrets,
He who doesn't know whether he loves me or hates me
like the scintillating news of faraway trips we long for
in childhood
leaving behind in a backdrop
with relief
when there comes a day in which we have no other choice
but to anchor our feet in remote, incurable geographies
in order to survive

In this region there are *wunderkinder*
proclaiming love and wisdom
I also tame lions and turn them into amusing cats
to give them a home outside the jungle
if they wish to come near me when I sleep

There are also secret hideaways, improvised shortcuts
to our vital happily-ever-after story endings
as we get increasingly close
to all the colors in the dancing pointillist façade
of this unbreakable canvas

Under the full moon
we give birth to songs and circular tales
feeding the bonfire
sliding in metallic cascades
over the ruins of ancient skyscrapers

I walk in the trail of primeval scent
and wind up in the sea
always the sea
reminding me of origins and sunrises
and the gift of wings

This is the voice of my circadian enemy
urging me
to flee no more
asking me
if he could look into my eyes

And I rejoice in the certainty of your arms
Holding me
in this bending moment
when the city melts down
like the froth of time.

LADY IN WHITE

In honor of Las damas de blanco, the Cuban peaceful women protesters

This lady has the longest arms
I've ever seen. She scrapes the skies
with gentle nails and dazzles from the glitter
of the stars. Bigger than those of legendary heroines,
her heart has grown its own heart
in confinement

Dressed in white like a bride,
a virgin, an African Goddess,
she's the peacekeeper's flag
standing on hunger strike until
her children are allowed to ignite
the air of the island with words of freedom

Scrutinizing the flash on the reporters' cameras,
I am the mediator. I am the messenger of tyrants
coming through, coming through, coming through
a procession of white roses and candles,
spiritual weapons silently seizing the colonial penitentiary
conjuring the strength of our ancestors to set her free

My mother,
she lets me look into her eyes and takes me back
to my childhood sprinkled with honey under tropical full moons
sacred as the sea

She wakes me up in the middle of nightmares
in our house of sun
and *yerbabuena*

My mother,
casting magic spells
at the vacant dinner table

My mother,
transubstantiating bread and wine
amidst Cuba's hysterical tempests and street stabbings

My mother,
Today
I need to be reborn from you

I throw myself into your arms
And become your baby boy again
Enveloped in the vortex of your womb.

AURORA

As if the tempest had seized my territory
Beast looking for bonanza

As if my hands secluded in forgotten nuances
Had found the treasure of the sailors

As if my timeless eyes
Had seen for the first time

I am new again to bonding promises of love
I am a man for all seasons

I am the singer who carries himself
With the dignity of forgotten manners

To reconcile the good
And the evil in my temple

Just whisper my name
Come and find me in the ruins of this castle

Miraculous man, you are the only one who knows
The antidote against oblivion and madness

When the world spins around
The witches' weaving looms.

THE FOOL ON BRONX PARK EAST

Of Rosewood the handle of his umbrella
I see him every day from Dusk to Dawn
flailing his skeleton umbrella under the sun
and the moon and the Milky Way
over the cars on the highway
almost naked
the bum
the man who never sleeps
unless
it's raining

He lives at the mercy of its sheltering frame
He has already surrendered to the honking of the cars
they stop to let him walk in his ragged underwear
giving them weather advice
drunk driving advice
parental advice and marriage counseling advice
the bum
the man who never sleeps
unless
it's raining

His umbrella is the remainder of a parachute
perhaps, left by an angel in his ascension to the skies
And the fool on Bronx Park East
aids the drivers bumper to bumper
opening and closing his skeleton umbrella
up and down the highways
the bum
the man who never sleeps
unless
it's raining

The umbrella and the umbrella man
have both lost their skin down to the bones
I am convinced he is the angel
who's lost his wings
and got stuck in New York
without a map of the heavenly skies
the bum
the man who never sleeps
unless
it's raining

The skeleton has resisted the corrosive action
of the elements
the man is attached to his umbrella
like an umbilical cord
limbically connected
to his bygone memory
the bum
the man who never sleeps
unless
it's raining

Is there, I ask myself, a need for skin
when you wear your soul inside out
protected
by the celestial
skeleton
of an umbrella?
the bum
the man who never sleeps
unless
it's raining

The Fool on Bronx Park East
run over by the siren
of a chasing highway patrol car
lets me handle and inspect his umbrella
while they dial 911
to save his skeleton
the bum
the man who never sleeps
unless
it's raining

"Make sure she's alright, buddy!"
he whispers
the highway is uncomfortably silent for a minute
a thousand headlights flashing
in the middle of the night
and then it rains, just for him
the bum
the man who never sleeps
unless
it's raining

The fool is gone
and I examine his umbrella
to make sure it's not been hurt
at his request
I examine his skeleton umbrella
the angel's parachute
that let him land
so low
so far from God
so close to the irony of life

And I am left alone
with the nose-cap, the collar, the tip cup
the hand-spring, the tube, the runner,
the inside rosette, the stopper pin, the stretcher,
the tip, the rib, the tie,
the prevent, the inside cap, the notch
the outside rosette, the open cap
the fit-up, the ferrule, the rosewood handle
The Umbrella, parachute to help me land
has grown its skin again; it's not a fragile frame.

WOMAN IN A PURPLE WIG

There she goes
She is leaning forward
On the merry-go-round
Spinning off into oblivion

Precarious equilibrium of the lonely
Where no one is available for love

Fast forward, her broken steps
On the unforgiving ground
Of her thousand setbacks

The woman in a purple wig
At eight o'clock in the morning
Is thrusting her bosom into the future
Her buttocks are running backwards
Into
Her
Smoggy
Foggy
Fuzzy
Past
Where she was once a mother's baby girl
Under orange full moons, lullabies, and nursery rhymes:
Come baby girl into your endless dream
Sleeping Beauty for all seasons

The woman in a purple wig is in a hurry
She fears someday she might wake up
And find her rapist, her preacher
And her dealer
In a corner of her life
Perpetuating the unfinished drama
Where she will learn
That she's become the anti-heroine
Trapped
At sunrise

The woman in a purple wig

There she goes
She pushes forward
Across the uncontainable ocean of *Atlantic Avenue*

With that innate nonsense of navigation
Bestowed upon shipwrecks

She is held by an invisible thread
To prevent her from plunging into the asphalt
Like an angel gone mad

Where are those places,
Portals to happiness
Where she was once loved?

The woman in a purple wig
Has been deceived by all
She won't hear the message
She won't have time to say goodbye
She won't be remembered

The woman in a purple wig

There she goes
On the merry-go-round
Spinning off into nowhere.

THE WORD

Fraught with subtle lies
you must be challenged
to reinvent your own alphabet
and find the word within
that's always been
the seed
of all wonders.

A teacher said that our Kingdom
was right here
amongst the persecuted
the cornered
the imprisoned
the tortured
amongst the ones
burned at the stake
for living by that word.

The problem is that false prophets
do not fear anything
but the word
emerging from your marrow to restore
Love
which has always been
in all languages
the most feared of all words.

I am Joe,
The Joey of my brother and sister
The Joy of my mother

I've collected all my belongings,
Carefully assorting them, first the crystal
Memories
The mirrors
Claimed by the ghosts of my ancestors

This house is FOR SALE

The aroma of coffee that followed me all the way from San Juan
When I was four
Is for sale
And my father's War Medals
Mom's Alzheimer's
Didn't break her
I cared for her
Until she ascended into the stars she'd shown me when I was her child
Mom, the only one who's loved me
Is in me; that's not for sale
Nor are Theresa's ashes
Cancer
Unearthed her.
The picture of my brother James
Who raped me until I was twelve
Is free with one condition
Burn it

Edgar, my lover of twenty years,
Is the color of these walls
My nemesis

This house is FOR SALE
With the ghosts that will never leave:
Pedro's son who killed himself in the attic
Smashed by heroin and coke,
Pedro, the father, who died of alcoholism
Right here

The whole family perished from uncertainties and old age
Cursed

They are buried here in the backyard by the pond
And they come out from time to time
Carrying the weight of their insanity
And they possess you and make you do very bad things until you lose it
This house is yours.

PENDULUM

Not Foucault's
But mine
And not necessarily the pendulum of my masculinity
And again, why not
If it's still there, still dictating consequences

Pendulum of the Baroque
Clocks on mysterious walls,
Magic Clocks

Pendulum that marks my old age,
I mean
My last earthly passport

Pendulum of all Cinderellas
Suffocated
By twelve strokes

Pendulum that bewitches
The tamed
Overwhelming shadow of Pavlov

Pendulum of all the clocks
In the pupils
Of Dali's melting eye

Pendulum
Of harlequins, courtesans
And Sunday clowns

Pendulum
Of the Big Ben
Witness of coronations and executions

Pendulum
Of trains, ships
And planes lost in the fog

Pendulum
Silent pendulum
of the tightrope

Pendulum
Of all Penelopes
Of all those who wait

Pendulum
Of those who never finish
Anything they start

Pendulum
Of the suicide's
Nightmares

Pendulum
Everlasting Pendulum I hold on to
In Faith

Pendulum
Of this blue ball
That gives us the sky

Pendulum, the caliber of life
The God's particle
That has made a pendulum out of me

I still let myself loose under tropical thunderstorms,
Lit by fireflies
And follow the smell of lilies
Pointing me
To the cup
Of coffee
Spoon
Pendulum of childhood
Already gone

Pendulum
Of the bells
John Donne's bells tolling for thee

The bells
Always portending bad omens:
Weddings, wars, deaths

But physicists know more
After all,
Physicists are the prophets of time and space
They are the ones who claim to have seen the shadow of God
And the tracks
That God always leaves behind.

STAR WITNESS

This morning
I have seen the highest mountains
burn down
adrift
cast away
propelled beyond the intrepid waters of this river
missing the distant blue
of remote lands carefully drafted by the child
bouncing off the walls
this child
who never stopped telling stories
even when the bad teacher
sour as a rotten orange
pulled him down from midair
and clipped his wings until the earlobes
hung limply like shredded bloody pendants in her crippled hands.

This morning
while seeking atonement
I have seen how the many names
inked in The Holy Scriptures
to disguise my Father
make it impossible to leave it all
in the hands of remembrance and forgiveness.

I have seen
how the wind with the help of water only
could freeze to dust
pyramids, mosques, synagogues and cathedrals
that no one would ever expunge from the collective consciousness.

Nothing will ever be completely extinguished
The Sphinx, The Nazca Lines,
Machu Picchu, Tikal, The Pyramids of Giza, Petra,
Stonehenge, The Parthenon, The Taj Mahal, The Roman Colosseum,
Angkor Wat,
Washington, D.C. imagined by the Masons,
Easter Island,
The Cathedral of San Cristóbal de La Habana,
are still looking at us with their cryptic eyes, engrossed,
demanding an answer.

I have seen
this morning, I have seen
how rising early is the best antidote
against the suicidal ideations of delirious nights.

This morning,
for the first time in over twenty years
I have seen myself in the mirror
and I have come to know
the love of God
still nesting in my earthly body.

This morning
is an awakening.

Like a butterfly hovering under the first ray of sun
I embrace
my resurrected
heart.